Crafts
of the
World

Mayan Weaving:
A Living Tradition

by Ann Stalcup

The Rosen Publishing Group's
PowerKids Press™
New York

To my husband Ed who shares my love of folk art and travel.

Published in 1999 by The Rosen Publishing Group, Inc.
29 East 21st Street, New York, NY 10010

First Edition

Book Design: Resa Listort

Photo Credits: pp. 4, 7, 10, 11, 13, 19 © JJ Foxx; p. 8 © Suzanne Murphy-Larronde/FPG International; p. 14 © Richard & Mary Magruder/ Viesti Associates, Inc.; p. 17 © Dr. Gerd Wagner/Viesti Associates Inc.

Stalcup, Ann, 1935–
    Mayan weaving : a living tradition / by Ann Stalcup.
       p.   cm. — (Crafts of the world)
    Includes index.
    Summary: Briefly describes how the Maya wove their cloth, how they dyed the fabric, and how they created the clothing they wore.
    ISBN 0-8239-5331-9
    1. Maya textile fabrics—Juvenile literature. 2. Weaving—Mexico—Juvenile literature. 3. Weaving—Central America—Juvenile literature. [1. Indian textile fabrics. 2. Mayas—Social life and customs. 3. Indians of Central America—Social life and customs. 4. Weaving.] I. Title. II. Series: Crafts of the world (PowerKids Press)
    F1435.3.T48S73 1998
    746'.089'97415—dc21
                                      98-5638
                                        CIP
                                        AC

Manufactured in the United States of America

Contents

The Maya

The ancient Maya were a people that lived in what we now call Mexico, Guatemala, and Honduras. Their **civilization** (sih-vih-lih-ZAY-shun) was most powerful between 250 and 900 AD. By about 1450, the ancient Maya had lost much of their land. Fortunately, Mayan villages still exist today.

The Maya planted cotton and **maize** (MAYZ), or corn. They spun the cotton into yarn. Then they wove beautiful **textiles** (TEK-stylz) with the yarn. In the 1500s Spanish **explorers** (ek-SPLOR-erz) brought sheep to the Maya from Europe. Wool comes from sheep. So the Maya started to weave with both cotton and wool. The Maya have been famous for the bright colors and beautiful designs in their weaving for hundreds of years.

◀ The Maya have been weaving beautiful cloth for over one thousand years!

Dyes

The cotton and wool that the Maya use are a tan color. To make their textiles bright, the Maya use dye to color the thread and the cloth. The first dyes were found in nature. Making the dyes was hard work. For hundreds of years, the women crushed **minerals** (MIH-nuh-rulz) and vegetable coloring in stone bowls to make dye. To make a deep-red dye, they would crush a tiny insect that they found in the desert. They made black dye from coal, yellow dye from parts of blackberry trees, and blue dye from a certain kind of clay.

In Mayan weaving each color stands for something. For example, yellow stands for maize, which is very important to the Maya. Yellow also stands for the sun. And red stands for life and energy.

The Maya often use many different ▶
bright colors in one cloth.

Designs

Cloth designs were often different from village to village. Some cloth made by Mayan weavers was decorated with **geometric** (jee-uh-MEH-trik) designs. Some cloths were striped and others had designs found in nature, such as flowers and animals.

The Maya **developed** (dih-VEH-lupt) a dying **technique** (tek-NEEK) known as *jaspe*. It is a lot like the tie-dying that many people do today. Bunches of yarn were tied tightly at certain spots, then dyed. The dye couldn't reach inside the tied sections. When the yarn dried and was untied, those sections stayed white. When woven, the undyed areas made a stripe across the cloth.

◀ Here you can see some of the many different colors and patterns created by Mayan weavers.

Weaving Methods

The Maya used the same weaving techniques for hundreds of years. Many are still used today. The weaver usually sits on the ground. One end of her **loom** (LOOM) is tied to a tree, and the other is tied around her back.

The loom has wooden rods at the top and bottom to hold the warp, or the long threads. A shuttle weaves thread back and forth through the warp threads. These threads are called the woof.

◀ Mayan girls are taught to weave when they are very young.

10

Mayan women no longer need to make their own dyes. ▶

Creating enough cloth for a piece of clothing can take as long as three months. The cotton and wool are spun, dyed, and then woven. Today Mayan women can buy different colored dyes. But in the past, when women made their own dyes, cloth-making took even longer.

Uses for Woven Cloth

In ancient times woven fabrics were often used to decorate Mayan **temples** (TEM-pulz). They were also worn as clothing. Because the weather was hot all year, Mayan clothing was simple. A man wore an *ex*, which was a cloth he wrapped around his hips. A woman wore a *kub*, which was a wraparound cotton skirt.

When the Spanish arrived in 1519, they brought the Catholic religion to the Maya. The Mayan religion began to change. Young women were taught to weave special heavy blouses called *huipils*. It became **traditional** (truh-DIH-shuh-nul) for a young Mayan woman to present the first *huipil* she wove to the spirit of a Catholic saint. The Maya believed that this would please the saint, who would look after them in the future.

Women still wear woven blouses and simple wraparound skirts. ▶

Changes in Mayan Clothing

What we think of as traditional Mayan clothing has only been worn by the Maya for the past 200 years. In 1770 women were ordered by the Spanish to cover their bodies from their necks all the way to their ankles. Many women began to weave Spanish-style blouses.

◀ Before the Spanish came, many Mayan women wore no shirts at all!

Ancient Mayan men wore Spanish-style shirts and loose pants. They carried shoulder bags and sometimes wore jackets. Wool or straw hats were not worn until the 1500s, when the Spanish first came from Europe. Then each Mayan village developed its own style of hat. Mayan children dressed like their parents.

Mayan children's clothes are just like grown-ups' clothes, ▶ except smaller.

Men's Roles in Weaving

Today the Maya live in small areas of Mexico and Guatemala. When Mayan men are not planting or picking crops, they weave or **crochet** (kroh-SHAY) shoulder bags. They often decorate them with geometric designs. The men carry their lunches, which are often wrapped in banana leaves, in these shoulder bags.

Using large looms brought from Europe by the Spanish, men weave cloth for women's wraparound skirts. Men also weave colorful **ponchos** (PON-chohz) that they wear themselves. Styles and colors are different from village to village. Some villages use lots of red. Others use lots of dark blue.

◄ The pouches that men weave, such as the one this man is wearing, are called *morales*.

Women's Costumes

Today colorful, handwoven clothes are a link to the Mayan **heritage** (HEHR-ih-tij). Women wear skirts, blouses, sashes, and sometimes **headdresses** (HED-dres-ez). Babies are tied to their mothers' backs with a rebozo, or long scarf.

Headdresses help hold cloth-wrapped bundles that Mayan women sometimes carry on their heads. The headdresses also show the region in which a woman lives. For example, in the Atitlan region of Guatemala, a woman will wrap a red strip around her head.

In some areas, a girl's headdress will change when the time comes for her to marry.

Weaving Project

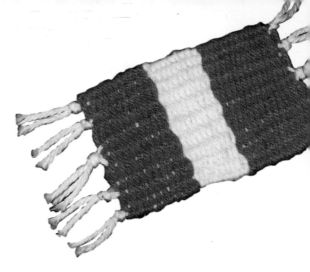

You Will Need:

- a heavy cardboard rectangle, about 6 inches by 8 inches
- brightly colored yarn (any color) cut into strings that are about nine feet long
- scissors
- ruler
- pencil

First you have to make your loom:

1. Draw a line across the cardboard about ½ inch below each of the six inch long ends.

2. Cut about eleven small "V" shapes into those two ends of the cardboard, equally spaced (about ½ inch apart).

3. About 7 inches from one end of the yarn, place the yarn in the first "V." Then wind the yarn around the cardboard by placing it in opposite "V"s once. When you are finished, leave about 7 inches of yarn at the end.

4. Tie the ends together in back, and cut off excess yarn. This is the warp.

Now you can weave:

1. Take a different colored yarn and tie the end to the top of the first warp yarn. (You can start on either side of the warp.)

2. Weave the yarn over and under the warp yarn, back and forth across the cardboard, until the warp is full. If you run out of yarn in the middle, or want to change colors, just tie the end of the yarn to the warp. Then tie the beginning of the new yarn to the warp where you left off and continue weaving. To finish your piece, tie the last bit of yarn to the last warp yarn.

3. Turn the loom over. Cut across the middle of the warp from one side to the other.

4. For a fringe: Tie each set of two yarns together on both ends of the woven project.

Today's Maya

Mayan people today live very much like the ancient Maya did. Many people still speak Mayan instead of Spanish.

But some things have changed since the days of the ancient Maya. Today factories spin Mayan cotton and wool into yarn. Even though the Maya still weave with cotton and wool, **synthetic** (sin-THEH-tik) yarns are used too. Synthetic dyes now make the colors that the Maya first found in nature. These dyes are easy to use and save a lot of time.

The weaving traditions begun by the ancient Maya are still alive today. Children in Mayan villages are learning to weave just as their parents and grandparents did. Their beautiful creations add to the rich **culture** (KUL-cher) of the Maya.

Glossary

civilization (sih-vih-lih-ZAY-shun) A group of people living in an organized and similar way.

crochet (kroh-SHAY) The looping and weaving of thread with a hooked needle.

culture (KUL-cher) The beliefs, customs, art, and religion of a people.

develop (dih-VEH-lup) To create and perfect.

explorer (ek-SPLOR-er) A person who travels and studies new places around the world.

geometric (jee-uh-MEH-trik) Made up of straight lines, circles, and other simple shapes.

headdress (HED-dres) A cloth or decoration worn on the head.

heritage (HEHR-ih-tij) The cultural traditions that are handed down from parent to child.

loom (LOOM) A tool for weaving yarn into cloth.

maize (MAYZ) The Spanish word for corn.

mineral (MIH-nuh-rul) Something, such as coal or copper, that comes from the ground that is not a plant, animal, or other living thing.

poncho (PON-choh) A woven blanket-like covering worn by Mayan men.

synthetic (sin-THEH-tik) Something that is not from nature; human-made.

technique (tek-NEEK) A way of doing something.

temple (TEM-pul) A place of worship.

textile (TEK-styl) Woven fabric or cloth.

traditional (truh-DIH-shuh-nul) To do things the way that a group has done them for a long time.

Index